MY ALLELUIA

Components available
35029719   Book
35029720   Book/Accompaniment CD

ISBN 978-1-4803-8698-3

SHAWNEE PRESS

EXCLUSIVELY DISTRIBUTED BY

HAL•LEONARD®
CORPORATION
7777 W. BLUEMOUND RD. P.O. BOX 13819 MILWAUKEE, WI 53213

In Australia Contact:
Hal Leonard Australia Pty. Ltd.
4 Lentara Court
Cheltenham, Victoria, 3192 Australia
Email: ausadmin@halleonard.com.au

Visit Shawnee Press online at
www.shawneepress.com

Dear Fellow Worshipper,

"My Alleluia" is more than just the title song of this collection. It is my worship. My own personal alleluia. This collection is not about a corporate time of congregational worship or a choir anthem sung by many voices. Each song began with me singing alone at my piano in my home. I'm amazed at how the writing process shines a spotlight into my soul: every piece was a spiritual journey of healing, conviction, grace, questions, remembrance, hope. So many pieces in this book have deeply personal stories behind them. It is truly *my* Alleluia.

In these pages, you will find songs that fit general worship times, as well as songs for different occasions. When possible, I've written some alternate cued notes for those of you who are low-voice singers – I'm an alto, and know how hard it can be to find songs that are comfortable to sing.

I pray that these pieces will minister to you and those around you, so that my alleluia can now become your alleluia!

Blessings,

Heather

HOME
(The Arms of God)

Words and Music by
HEATHER SORENSON (ASCAP)

in honor of the 10th anniversary of the Alleluia Conference at Baylor University, July 19-22, 2011

MY ALLELUIA

Words and Music by
HEATHER SORENSON (ASCAP)

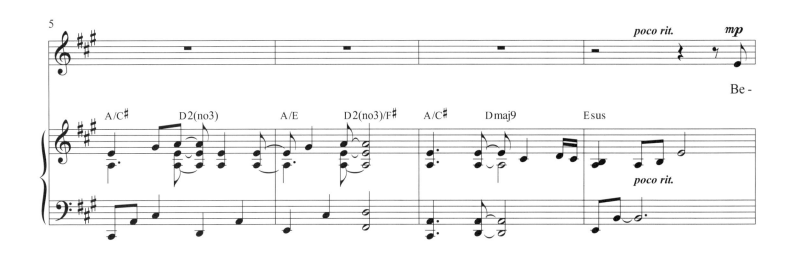

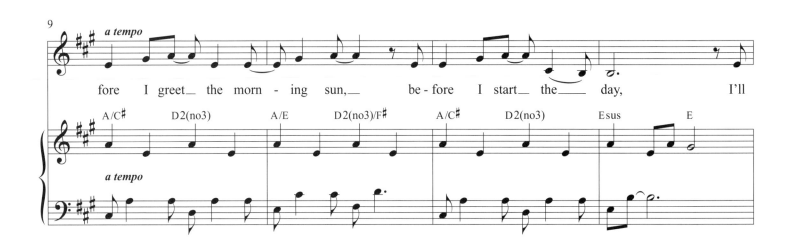

MERCY STILL

Words by
CHARLES WESLEY (1707-1788)

Music by
NICOLE ELSEY
Arranged by
HEATHER SORENSON (ASCAP)

30
I a-gain have cru-ci-fied, and pro-faned His hal-lowed name;

34
put Him to an o - pen shame. There, for me, the Sav - ior stands; shows His

38
wounds, and spreads His hands. God is love! I know, I feel. Oh,—

42
Je - sus weeps and loves me still, loves me still!

poco rit.

Now in - cline me to re - pent. Let me__ now my__ sins la - ment;

live in grace and be re-stored; weep, be - lieve, and__ sin no more. Depth of

mer - cy, can there be mer-cy still re-served for me? God is

love! I know, I feel. Oh,__ Je - sus__ weeps and loves me

still! Is there mer - cy still?_____ Is there mer - cy still?_____

_____ There is mer - cy still._____ Yes, there's mer - cy still._____

_____ There is mer - cy_____ still for me._____

ROCK OF AGES
(Forgiven and Free)

Words by
HEATHER SORENSON (ASCAP)
and AUGUSTUS M. TOPLADY (1740-1778)

Music by
HEATHER SORENSON (ASCAP)

Relaxed Contemporary Gospel (♩ = ca. 64)

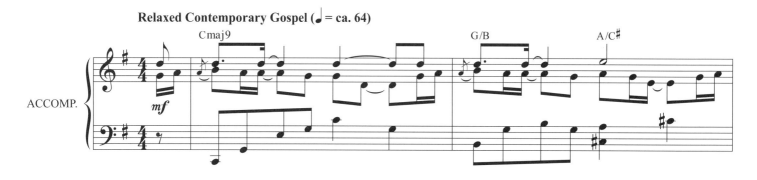

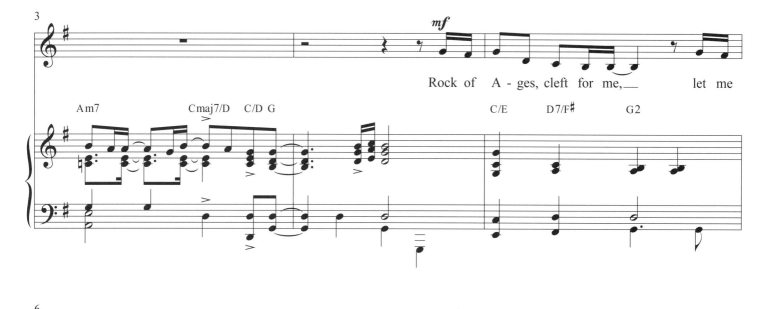

Rock of A - ges, cleft for me,___ let me

hide my - self in Thee.___ Let the wa - ter and___ the blood, from Your

save, and Thou a - lone. Noth-ing in my hands_ I bring, sim-ply

to Your cross_ I cling._____ Hal - le - lu - jah, I'm_____ for-giv - en and free!_____

I was lost un - til_____ You found_ me, I was

blind but now_____ I see;_____ Hal - le - lu - jah, I'm_____ for-giv - en and free!_____

* Tune: TOPLADY, Thomas Hastings, 1784-1872

for Julien Wilbur Jamar

CHRISTMAS DREAMS

Words by
HEATHER SORENSON (ASCAP)
inspired and adapted from the anonymous poem
"Miracle Dreams"

Music by
HEATHER SORENSON (ASCAP)

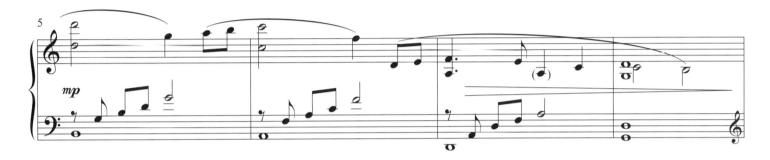

On that Christ-mas night when mys-tic stars shone bright, a

wist-ful blind man moved in sleep, and dreamed that he had sight. That

17
a tempo

night when shep - herds heard an an - gel choir____ near, a

21
poco rit.

deaf man stirred in slum-ber's spell, and dreamed that he could hear.

25
p a tempo

Child of heal - ing, Child of__ hope, take the things that hurt us most, and

29
poco rit.

with Your touch they'll be re - deemed, Ho - ly Child of Christ-mas

48 *a tempo*　　　　　　　　　　　　　　　　　　　　　　*mf*

night when o'er　the Babe,　　young Ma - ry rose　to lean,　　　a

52　　　　　　　　　　　　　　　　　　　　　　*rit.*

loath - some lep - er smiled in sleep　and dreamed that he was— clean.

56　*f a tempo*

Child of heal - ing, Child　of— hope,　take the things that　hurt us most,　and

60

with　Your touch,　they'll be re - deemed,　Ho - ly Child　of Christ - mas—

Child of heal - ing, Child of hope, take the things that hurt us most, and

with Your touch they'll be re - deemed, Ho - ly Child of Christ - mas

dreams. Ho - ly Child of Christ - mas dreams.

COME, THOU FOUNT OF EVERY BLESSING

Words from
Wyeth's *Repository of Sacred Music, Part Second*, 1813

Tune: **NETTLETON**
by ROBERT ROBINSON (1735-1790)
Arranged by
HEATHER SORENSON (ASCAP)

for Jachin Micah Johnston

LULLABY PRAYER
(A Prayer for Children)

Words and Music by
HEATHER SORENSON (ASCAP)

pres - ence near; give them peace, help them sleep._____ And

if their path goes through the cold, in Your arms please en - fold.

Show them that Your love can melt fro - zen hearts, fro - zen souls.

Help them grow when there's no rain, free their hearts where they've been chained;

noise that drowns out Your com-mands. Hold their hand, help them stand.

So bless these lit-tle

chil-dren, Lord, ti-ny souls so a-dored. Lit-tle lambs to You be-long.____

They are weak,____ but You are strong.

for the Lavon Drive Baptist Church Worship Choir

TURN AROUND AND SEE

Words and Music by
HEATHER SORENSON (ASCAP)
Incorporating
"He Leadeth Me"

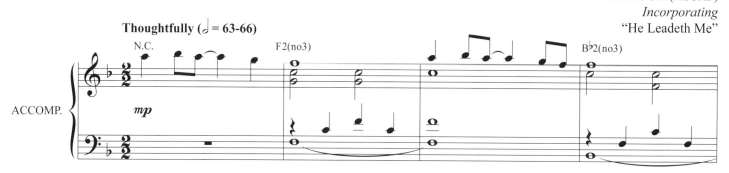

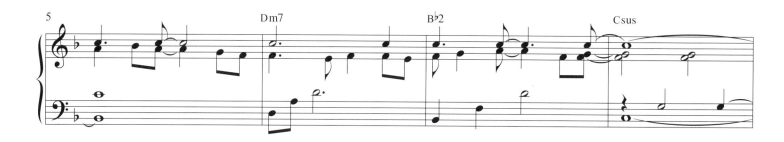

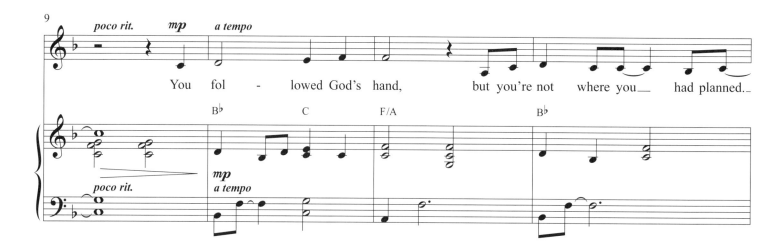

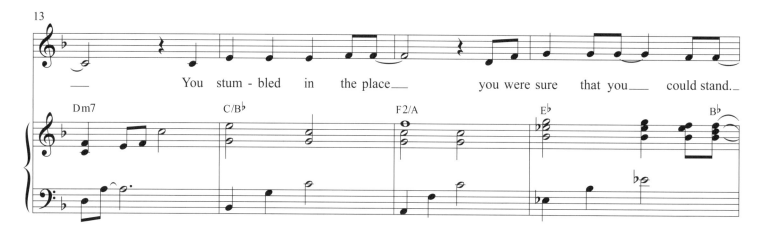

turn a-round___ and___ see.___

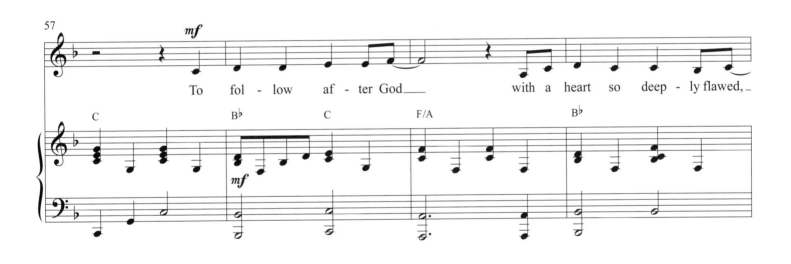

To fol - low af - ter God___ with a heart so deep - ly flawed,

___ be a light in the dark,___ yet so oft - en miss the mark;

* Tune: HE LEADETH ME, Joseph H. Gilmore, 1834-1918
  Words: William B. Bradbury, 1816-1868

STAINED GLASS

Words by
JOSEPH M. MARTIN (BMI)

Music by
HEATHER SORENSON (ASCAP)

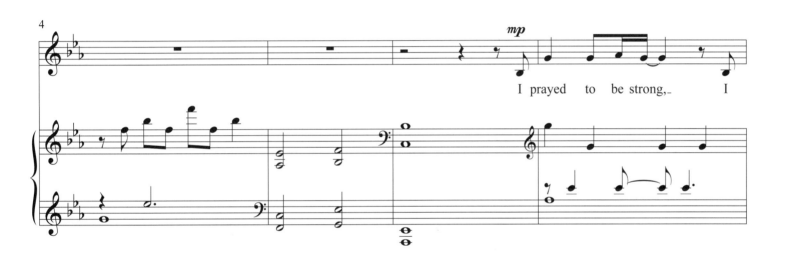

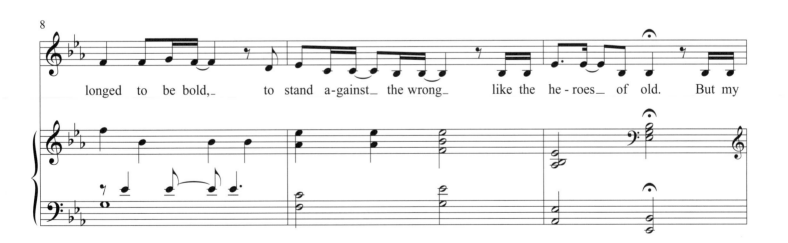

for the Lavon Drive Baptist Church Worship Choir, Garland, Texas

RAISE YOUR HANDS

Words and Music by
HEATHER SORENSON (ASCAP)

Raise your_____ hands when you're high up-on_____ the moun-

- tain,_____ and you know that you've_ been blessed._ Raise your_____

hands when you start your day_ with noth - ing,_____ and you end with e - ven less._

want to claim as yours.___ Raise your_____ hands,

reach - ing up___ to heav - en___ when your heart's bowed to the floor.___

Raise your_____ hands, trust - ing in___ the grace___ of God___ that has

car - ried you be - fore._____ I will lift___ my

hands to You, and bless Your name_ for - ev - er. I will lift_ my

hands to You and bless Your ho - ly name. I will lift_ my

hands to You and bless Your name_ for - ev - er. I will lift_ my

hands to You and bless Your ho - ly name._

molto rit.